PERU

Lost Cities, Found Hopes

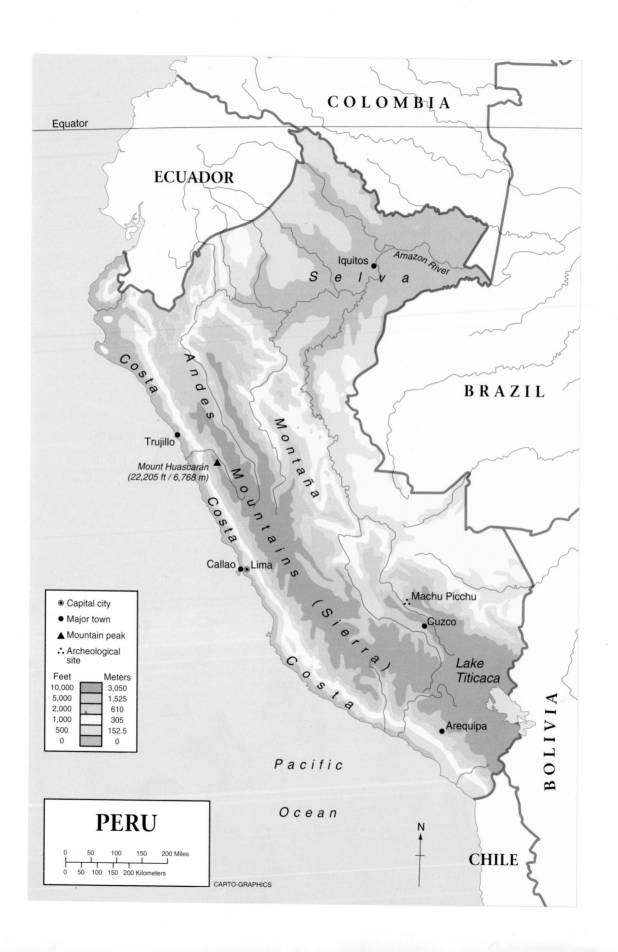

COLOMBIA

Equator

ECUADOR

Iquitos •   *Amazon River*

S e l v a

BRAZIL

Trujillo •

C o s t a

A n d e s

Mount Huascarán ▲
(22,205 ft / 6,768 m)

M o u n t a i n s

M o n t a ñ a

Callao •   ⊙ Lima

Machu Picchu ∴

Cuzco •

(S i e r r a)

*Lake
Titicaca*

C o s t a

⊙ Capital city
● Major town
▲ Mountain peak
∴ Archeological
   site

Feet	Meters
10,000	3,050
5,000	1,525
2,000	610
1,000	305
500	152.5
0	0

Arequipa •

BOLIVIA

P a c i f i c

O c e a n

N

PERU

0   50   100   150   200 Miles

0   50 100 150 200 Kilometers

CHILE

CARTO-GRAPHICS

EXPLORING CULTURES OF THE WORLD

PERU

Lost Cities, Found Hopes

David C. King

BENCHMARK BOOKS

MARSHALL CAVENDISH
NEW YORK

The publisher would like to thank Karen Spalding, Professor of History at the University of Connecticut, for her expert review of the manuscript.

Benchmark Books
Marshall Cavendish Corporation
99 White Plains Road
Tarrytown, New York 10591-9001

© Marshall Cavendish Corporation 1998

Library of Congress Cataloging-in-Publication Data
King, David C.
    Peru : lost cities, found hopes / by David C. King.
        p.   cm. — (Exploring cultures of the world)
    Includes bibliographical references and index.
    Summary: Examines the geography, history, government, people, and culture of Peru.
    ISBN 0-7614-0396-5 (lib. binding)
    1. Peru—Civilization—Juvenile literature. [1. Peru.] I. Title. II. Series.
    F3410.K56   1998
    985—dc21

                                                        97-2722
                                                        CIP
                                                        AC

Printed in Hong Kong

Series design by Carol Matsuyama

Front cover: A child dressed in traditional clothing plays an Andean flute.
Back cover: A group of school girls on the coast of Peru.

Photo Credits
Cover: ©Steve Vidler/Leo de Wys, Inc.; Back cover and pages 6, 11, 23, 24, 27, 28, 31, 37, 40, 42, 43, 46, 48, 53: ©Beryl Goldberg; Title page and pages 18, 55: ©Frank and Helen Schreider/National Geographic Society; page 9: ©Inga Spence/DDB Stock Photo; page 13: ©Robert Frerck/Woodfin Camp & Associates, Inc.; page 15: Bridgeman/Art Resource, NY; page 20: ©Jerry Liebman/Leo de Wys, Inc., NY; page 25: Mauricio Anjel/International Stock; pages 32-33, 34, 39: ©William A. Allard/National Geographic Society; page 50: ©Richard Perry/National Geographic Society; page 51: John Bigelow Taylor/American Museum of Natural History, #5060; page 52: ©Douglas Mason/Woodfin Camp & Associates, Inc.

Contents

The city of Cuzco was once the capital of the great Inca Empire.

1
GEOGRAPHY AND HISTORY

Peru Past and Present

"The One Who Makes the Earth Tremble"

In 1437, the small empire of the Inca was in grave danger. The powerful Chanca Indian tribe was marching on the city of Cuzco, the capital of the empire. The aging emperor, who was the ruler of the Inca people, felt he could not stop the attack, and he fled the city. The emperor's oldest son, the heir to the throne, also failed to act. The emperor's youngest son, however, a twenty-year-old named Yupanqui, was willing to take charge of the city's defense.

According to Inca legend, Yupanqui had a vision. He imagined the figure of a man with serpents wrapped around his arms and a puma, or mountain lion, across his shoulders. The man showed him a mirror that reflected all the lands Yupanqui would conquer if he defended Cuzco.

Yupanqui obeyed the vision and organized a brilliant defense of the city. The victory saved Cuzco and the Inca Empire. The grateful people gave their hero Yupanqui the new name of Pachacuti, which means "the one who makes the earth tremble." Pachacuti strengthened his army, pursued the Chanca, and overwhelmed them in another great battle. The next year, in 1438, Pachacuti seized power from his father and brother and became emperor of the Inca.

As emperor, Pachacuti launched an amazing campaign of conquest. Over a thirty-year period, the new emperor and his son, Topa Inca, conquered kingdom after kingdom, extending the boundaries of Inca rule both north and south. At its peak, the Inca Empire stretched 2,500 miles (4,023 kilometers) along the coast of South America.

Pachacuti was a brilliant ruler. He expanded the city of Cuzco and oversaw the construction of massive stone temples and palaces. He established Quechua, the Inca language, as the official language that was spoken throughout the empire. Having one language made it easier to rule efficiently over an estimated 12 million subjects.

Pachacuti's engineers built 10,000 miles (16,093 kilometers) of roads through the Andes Mountains. Well-designed rope bridges crossed rivers and breathtaking mountain chasms. Imperial runners, stationed at seven-mile intervals, carried messages over the roads at a rate of more than 200 miles a day. Inca temples and palaces were decorated with dazzling ornaments and furnishings in hand-wrought gold and silver.

Unfortunately, Pachacuti's great empire did not last long. Soon after the death of his son, Topa Inca, there was a struggle for power among his grandsons. In 1532, a small force of Spaniards invaded and, within a year, conquered the Inca armies. Although the great age of the Inca lasted only a century, modern Peruvians feel a deep pride in the rich civilization of the Inca. Peru's language, customs, and arts continue to reflect the influence of that great age, when Pachacuti made the earth tremble.

Mountains, Desert, and Rain Forest

The land that was once the heart of the Inca Empire is now Peru, the third-largest nation in South America. (Only Brazil and Argentina are larger.) Peru covers an area about three times the size of the state of California, but it has fewer people.

The spectacular snow-peaked Andes overlook a farming village near Cuzco.

On the north, Peru is bordered by Ecuador and Colombia. Brazil and Bolivia lie to the east, while Chile lies along the southern border. To the west is the Pacific Ocean.

Peru is a country of dramatic geographic contrasts. The towering, snow-capped Andes Mountains run through the center of the country from north to south. To the west of the mountains, along the coast, a narrow belt of flat land extends the length of the country. This coastal plain has one of the driest climates in the world. East of the Andes Mountains is the steamy Amazon rain forest. In the southern part of the country lies Lake Titicaca, which Peru shares with Bolivia. The lake is more than two miles above sea level, which makes it the world's highest body of water that can be navigated by ship.

Peru is in the Southern Hemisphere—the half of the earth that is below the equator. For this reason, the seasons occur at different times of the year than they do in Europe and North America, which are north of the equator. For example, spring arrives in Peru in November.

The *Costa*

About two-thirds of Peru's people live on the narrow coastal strip, which is called the *costa*. Although the northernmost point of the *costa* isn't far from the equator, the temperatures are moderate throughout the year. The cold waters of the Peru Current—a water movement in the South Pacific Ocean—flow along the coast, producing average temperatures that range from 66 degrees Fahrenheit (19 degrees Celsius) in winter to only 72 degrees Fahrenheit (22 degrees Celsius) in summer. The very dry coastal climate is caused by the Andes Mountains. Rain-bearing winds from the east are blocked by the Andes, creating desert conditions on the coast. Fortunately, irrigation has allowed large areas of the desert to be turned into rich farmland.

All of Peru's major cities are located in the *costa* region. The largest city by far is Lima, with more than six million people. The southern city of Arequipa is the second-largest. Callao, just west of Lima, is the country's largest port.

Peru's coastal waters are rich in bird, fish, and marine mammal life. Great herds of sea lions share rocky coastal islands with flocks of gulls, cormorants, pelicans, and the endangered Humboldt penguins.

The *Sierra*

The region of the Andes Mountains is known as the *sierra*. It covers about 27 percent of Peru. The mountains are very high. Mt. Huascarán, the tallest peak, rises more than 22,000 feet (6,700 meters). The Andes were formed by the collision of two plates, or sheets of rock in the earth's crust. These plates are still moving, and their movement creates earthquakes. While most earthquakes in this region are minor, some have caused wide-

Much of the farmland in the sierra is terraced, like this land near Arequipa.

spread destruction. One that occurred in 1970 resulted in more than 60,000 deaths. Indian groups, the descendants of the Inca, live in farm villages scattered throughout the *sierra*. The climate in these villages varies depending on their altitude. It is generally colder at the higher elevations.

The *Montaña* and *Selva*

To the east, the lower slopes of the Andes Mountains form a heavily forested region called the *montaña* (mon-TAHN-ya). Its lower part, known as the *selva*, or jungle, is a land of tropical rain forests and mighty rivers. The powerful Amazon, South America's longest river, begins in the *selva*.

The *montaña* and the *selva* together cover nearly two-thirds of Peru's land area, but the thick forests make this the least populated part of the nation. Isolated groups of Indians, divided into nearly forty small tribes, live in the Amazon rain forest. The rain forest is also the home of a great variety of plant and animal species. Mammals include the jaguar, tapir (which looks like a pig), and many varieties of monkeys. The rain forest is also home to the capybara—the world's largest rodent, reaching lengths of up to four feet. The hot, moist air of the forest is filled with the buzz of insects, the chatter of monkeys, and the notes of songbirds. Some of the quietest residents of the *selva* are the snakes, which slide noiselessly through the dense jungle growth.

The World of the Inca

Much of Peru's early history is shrouded in mystery. At one time there were several ancient civilizations in Peru, some dating back more than 2,000 years. A number of these early societies left impressive stone ruins. The people displayed great skill in weaving cloth, making pottery, and working with gold and silver. The early peoples of Peru were also farmers. They were the first in the world to cultivate potatoes, which became popular in Europe after 1500 and are now a basic food in many countries.

When Pachacuti took the throne as the ninth ruler of the Inca in 1438, he ruled what was then only one of several highly advanced kingdoms. As a result of his conquests, and those of his son Topa Inca, these kingdoms were joined together. They became the great Inca Empire.

These ruins are a reminder of the splendors of the Inca Empire, which was conquered by the Spanish in the 1530s.

With an elaborate system of roads and a common language to help unite the people, the Inca ruled their empire with remarkable efficiency. Every family had to contribute part of its crops to the emperor and to the sun god, Inti. In return, the emperor made certain that everyone had shelter, clothing, and an abundance of food. People with special skills were encouraged to work as stone masons, metal workers, weavers, or potters.

The great wealth of the Inca Empire, however, helped to cause its downfall. Only a few years after Topa Inca's death, the greed of his grandsons drove them to fight one another for political control in what became a bloody civil war. The fighting so weakened the empire that it easily fell to Spanish conquerors. The Spanish had been lured to Peru by stories of cities filled with gold and silver.

Spanish Rule

The Spanish conquest was led by Francisco Pizarro. He invaded the Inca Empire in 1532. With him was an army of only 180 men. The Inca soldiers far outnumbered the Spanish invaders. Their spears, however, were no match for the guns of the Spanish army—or their horses, two marvels the Inca had never seen before. Pizarro used trickery to capture and murder the Inca ruler, and the empire—beset for years by civil war—quickly fell to the foreign invaders.

The Spaniards built the city of Lima on the coast so that they could easily ship their plundered gold and silver to Spain. They forced many Indians to work in their gold and silver mines. Spanish colonists took over large pieces of land, and they used some of the Inca people to work for them on their plantations.

Spanish conqueror Francisco Pizarro seizes the Inca ruler, and the empire falls to the invaders.

Although many Inca farmers were able to keep their land, they were forced to pay tribute to the colonial state. The Indians suffered greatly at the hands of the Spanish. The colonists unknowingly brought diseases, such as smallpox, that were new to the Inca. Because they had no resistance to these diseases, the Indians died in great numbers. Within a short time after the conquest, 80 percent of the Inca had died.

Thousands of Spaniards immigrated to Peru. Some came as missionaries to convert the Indians to Christianity. Others came to establish businesses or to enjoy the wealth of a large plantation. Peru quickly became the wealthiest and most important colony in Spain's New World empire, which covered most of Central and South America. The society of colonial Peru was dominated by this small upper class of Spaniards, whose descendants are sometimes called Creoles, or *Criollos*. The Indians lived in grinding poverty as farm workers, called *campesinos*.

In addition to the Indians and the Creoles, a new race of people, called mestizos (meh-STEE-zohz) emerged during the three centuries of Spanish rule. Mestizos are of Indian and Spanish ancestry, the result of intermarriage between the two groups. The mestizos gradually became Peru's middle class, working in business and minor government jobs. The division of Peru into these three groups continues today.

Independence and the Struggle for Democracy

In the early 1800s, movements for independence swept through Spain's New World empire. In South America, the struggle for liberation from Spain was led by two Creoles. José de San Martín helped to win independence in the southern part of the continent, and Simón Bolívar led struggles in the north. Both men were active in gaining Peru's independence, which was declared by San Martín in 1821 and finally won by Bolívar's army in 1824.

Over the nearly two centuries since they won independence from Spain, the people of Peru have struggled to create a stable economy and a lasting democracy. Periods of democratic government have repeatedly been replaced by military dictatorships. And Peru is still a land in which a small number of wealthy people hold the reins of power while the great majority are poor.

In spite of these problems, some reforms have been made over the past thirty years. Many plantations, or haciendas,

THE GOVERNMENT OF PERU

Peru is officially a republic. The president, however, has broad powers to set aside the Constitution and rule as a dictator.

There are three branches of government. The executive branch is headed by the president, who is elected for a five-year term. The legislative, or law-making, branch is made up of two houses: the Senate, with 60 members, and the Chamber of Deputies, with 180 members. The Supreme Court is the highest court in the judicial branch. The court's 16 justices are chosen by the president.

The country is divided into 24 departments. In addition, there is one province called Callao. Unlike states in the United States, the departments do not have the power to govern themselves. Instead, they serve as administrative units for the national government.

All citizens may vote when they reach the age of eighteen.

have been turned into farm cooperatives owned by the Indians. Hundreds of schools have been built, and efforts are being made to extend education into the more remote Indian villages of the *sierra* and *montaña*.

Democratic elections were held once more in 1980. In 1990, Alberto Fujimori, a Peruvian of Japanese descent, was elected president. He was re-elected in 1995. Fujimori says that he is dedicated to democracy and economic reform. He has nevertheless frequently set aside the Constitution and used emergency, dictatorial powers to put down revolutionary movements. There are several revolutionary groups in Peru, and political unrest continues. In spite of these problems, many Peruvians are hopeful that one day their struggle for a true democracy will succeed.

A Quechua Indian from the mountains of southern Peru carries her baby on her back and a young animal in her arms.

2
THE PEOPLE

The Many Faces
of Peru

Deep in the tropical rain forest, a family of Amazonian Indians burns away a patch of trees to clear space for planting crops. Far to the west, Andean Indians in colorful ponchos herd their llamas and alpacas on a steep mountainside. On the coast, in Lima, a husband and wife drive through heavy traffic to their downtown offices. All of these people are Peruvians, although their clothing, way of life, and even their language are different. Peru is a nation of both Indian and Spanish ancestry. These two strands have been mixing for nearly 500 years, but they have never completely blended.

Spanish, Indians, and Mestizos

Since colonial times, Peru's government and economy have been controlled by people of Spanish descent. They make up about 15 percent of Peru's population of nearly 24 million people. While most live in the cities, smaller numbers still live on haciendas in the *costa* region.

Almost half of the nation's population is Indian. Although many have moved to Lima and other cities, most still live in isolated villages in the Andes Mountains. The majority of Indians speak both Spanish and Quechua (ket-CHOO-ah), the ancient language of the Inca. Those who live in the south around Lake Titicaca speak Aymara, another ancient language, rather than Quechua.

In the Amazon rain forest, some small tribes of Indians have almost no contact with the outside world. Protected by the dense jungle growth, they never became part of the Inca Empire. Most of these tribes live by farming small plots of

Like other Indians of the rain forest, this father and his children wear traditional clothing and body paint.

SAY IT IN QUECHUA, SAY IT IN SPANISH

The majority of Peruvians speak both Spanish and one Indian language, which is usually Quechua. Here are some words and phrases in Quechua and Spanish:

How are you?	Quechua: *Imaynalla?* (ee-mee-NAL-ya)
	Spanish: *Cómo está usted?* (COH-moh es-TAH oo-STEHD)
I'm fine.	Quechua: *Allinmi.* (al-YIN-mee)
	Spanish: *Estoy bien.* (ehs-TOY bee-EHN)
Please come in.	Quechua: *Yaykurimuy.* (yee-koo-REE-mwee)
	Spanish: *Está en su casa.* (es-TAH EHN SOO CAH-sah)
	(This actually means "You are in your house" and is used as a welcome.)
Yes	Quechua: *Ari* (ah-REE)
	Spanish: *Sí* (SEE)
No	Quechua: *Mana* (MA-nah)
	Spanish: *No* (NO)

land. Others are nomads who move often in search of wild foods and game. Even the Amazonian farm families move often. The rain-forest soil loses nutrients when exposed to the sun, and these families must look for new soil to cultivate.

About 37 percent of Peru's people are mestizos. To a great extent, they make up the nation's middle class. Many work for government agencies, while others are active in business, crafts, health care, and education.

People of African or Asian descent make up less than 5 percent of the population. Alberto Fujimori's election to the

21

presidency is one sign that people of non-Spanish descent are now more widely accepted than they were in the past. There continues to be prejudice against the Indian population, however. Much of this is because many Indians do not speak Spanish and only a few attend schools.

Life in the Country

In the rugged highlands of the Andes Mountains, Indian families face a hard life in a difficult environment. Many Indians plant their crops on terraced hillsides, where the land rises in a series of steps. A lot of these terraces were carved by the Inca more than five centuries ago. Some of the farm villages are at altitudes of 15,000 feet above sea level. Only in the Himalayan Mountains of Asia do people live at such dizzying heights. Andean farmhouses are simple huts with adobe, or mud-brick, walls and thatched roofs. While some of the larger towns have electricity, there is no running water. Most families use llamas and alpacas to carry light burdens. The fleece, or woolly coat, of these camel-like animals is spun into yarn.

While large numbers of Andean Indians have migrated to Lima, many have also moved to the irrigated lowlands of the *costa*. There they live on haciendas owned by either Spanish landlords or by several Indian families as a cooperative. On the *costa* farms, Peruvians grow coffee, sugarcane, rice, cotton, corn, grapes, and a variety of vegetables. With the help of irrigation, crop yields are much higher than in the *sierra*. The farms on the *costa* therefore produce much of the food sold in Peru's cities. With electricity and running water, living conditions in the *costa* are much more modern than in the Andes.

Some of the Indians who live in the Andes Mountains keep small flocks of sheep like these.

Farm workers harvest potatoes in the Urubamba River Valley near Cuzco. Ancient Peruvians were the first people to grow potatoes.

Far to the east, in the dense Amazon rain forest, there is only a little room for farming. The nearly forty Indian tribes add to the production of their small farm plots by fishing and gathering wild foods. These tribes live in houses made of bamboo poles and thatched roofs.

City Life

About 70 percent of Peru's people live in cities. The nation's capital, Lima, is by far the largest city. Nearly one-third of the country's population lives in this huge, crowded metropolis. Its tall, earthquake-proofed office buildings and apartments overshadow the colonial churches and mansions below.

Groups of industrial buildings line the roads going west from Lima, all the way to the port of Callao on the coast. There are so many suburbs stretching in all directions that many residents of Lima call their city *El Pulpo*, or "the Octopus."

In the city, many men and women work in government offices, banks, law firms, manufacturing industries, and retail stores. They live in modern apartments or in suburban homes with small lawns or enclosed courtyards.

In contrast to the busy, prosperous parts of the city are Lima's shantytowns, settlements of crudely built homes. About one-half of Lima's people live in poverty. These are the newcomers—mostly Indians from the *sierra*—lured to the city by dreams of jobs and better lives. But jobs are hard to find, especially for people with little schooling and no special skills.

The bustling city of Lima contains almost one-third of Peru's population.

The shantytowns ring the outskirts of the city. The dwellings are made of scrap wood and cardboard, with sheets of tin for roofs. Many settlements, which are called *pueblo jóvenes*, or "young towns," lack basic necessities, such as electricity and running water. A lot of the newcomers eventually find work in the small assembly plants and handicraft shops that have sprung up in these towns. Government programs offer some financial assistance, and more schools are being built for both adults and children.

In addition to Lima, Peru's smaller cities and many towns are also growing rapidly. Some cities serve special purposes. Callao, for example, is the country's major seaport and the center of the fish-processing industry. Peru has one of the world's largest fishing industries. Enormous catches of anchovies and sardines are made into fish meal, which is sold worldwide as livestock feed. Other small cities are located in mining regions, where copper, lead, iron, and other metals are extracted.

The Blending of Religions

When the Spanish conquered the Inca Empire in the 1530s, they imposed the Roman Catholic religion on the many tribes in the empire. Today, 95 percent of Peru's people are Roman Catholic. The Andean Indians, however, never forgot the rich heritage of their native religions. Over the centuries, they have combined Christian beliefs with those of the Inca and other early religions. In celebrating a Catholic holy day, for example, an Andean community will combine church ritual with ceremonies in honor of the gods of the harvest.

In the cities, the religious services follow traditional Catholic practices more closely. Peruvians were given freedom

A group of Boy Scouts stands in front of a Roman Catholic church in Lima. Most Peruvians are Catholic.

of religion in 1979, and this has led to the growth of several Protestant and Evangelical churches. There are also a small number of Jewish synagogues and Buddhist temples.

In all its variations, religion remains important in the daily life of all Peruvians. Most major holidays are religious holy days, and many towns have special festivals to honor their patron saints or to celebrate a combination of Christian and Indian observances.

A Peruvian family in Lima, ready for a Sunday outing.

3

FAMILY LIFE, FESTIVALS, AND FOOD

Different Ways of Life

Throughout Peru, the family unit is very important. The husband is regarded as the unquestioned head of the family. He is responsible for providing for the family, while the wife is expected to manage the household and care for the children. In practice, however, women exercise a strong influence on all family decisions. In addition, a growing number of women in the cities work outside the home. In farming communities, women often work in the fields with the men.

How a family lives, and how well it lives, depends on whether the family lives in the city or the country.

Urban Families

Except for the newcomers in the shantytowns, most city families live comfortably. Children and their parents often live with their grandparents in the same household. Their apartment or house is modern and well furnished. The clothing they wear would look familiar to a visitor from the United States or Canada.

Most urban women continue their traditional roles as wives and mothers, but a growing number have jobs outside the home as well. Women now make up about one-quarter of the workforce. Both men and women workers put in a long work week. Businesses are open six days a week, and many stores are open on Sunday as well.

Urban parents are eager to give their children every possible advantage. Those who can afford to, for example, send their children to private schools, which have smaller classes than public schools. Some of the wealthiest families even arrange marriages for their sons and daughters.

Rural Indian Families

Life is much harder for Indian families in the highlands of the Andes. An extended family, which includes grandparents, aunts, uncles, and cousins, is likely to live together in a group of small adobe huts. Each family eats and sleeps in its own one-room hut, but the families prepare meals together in a separate building used only for cooking. There is no electricity or indoor plumbing. Water is carried in buckets from the nearest stream.

In the spring, men and women go to the fields together to plant the corn, potatoes, beans, and native grains. The men turn over the soil with old wooden hoes, and the women drop in the seeds. Children tend the llamas, alpacas, or sheep, which are raised for their wool. In many families, everyone shares in the work of cleaning, combing, and dyeing the wool. In some families, everyone helps in knitting or weaving the wool into beautiful cloth for sweaters, ponchos, shawls, and blankets. In other families, only the women are the weavers.

In the Andes, women knit or wind yarn into balls. Peruvian Indians are known for their skillful knitting and weaving.

Holidays and Festivals

Peruvians enjoy a variety of national holidays, Catholic holy days, and regional festivals, called *ferias*. One of the most beautiful *ferias* is held in the mountain city of Cuzco, the ancient capital of the Inca. This celebration is held around the time of the winter solstice, when the sun lies low in the horizon. The winter solstice falls on June 21 in the Southern Hemisphere. The holiday combines ancient Inca and Roman Catholic traditions. The Inca part of the festival, called *Inti Raymi*, honors the sun-god Inti. The Catholic holy day that is celebrated is the Feast of Corpus Christi.

31

Large crowds gather on the stone ruins of ancient Inca walls to watch a long procession of Andean Indians dressed in brilliant red or blue tunics. On their heads, the Indians wear tall red or black headdresses. Flutes and drums play a steady, repeating rhythm over and over. This pageant, which lasts several days, is meant to guarantee that the sun will again rise high in the southern sky. On each day of the pageant, a Mass is celebrated in the Catholic cathedral. The cathedral is built on the foundations of the ancient Inca temple. Each day's ceremonies conclude with a feast, horse races, music, and ritual dances.

Every region of the Andes has its own holiday,

Indians march in colorful procession in Cuzco's yearly celebration of Inti Raymi *and the Feast of Corpus Christi. The festival combines the traditions of the Inca and the Spanish.*

which usually combines a celebration of the town's patron saint with ancient Inca or other tribal observances. Many towns have nonreligious festivals as well. The northern city of Trujillo, for example, is one of many communities that holds a folk dance competition in the summer and a dance festival in the spring.

Worshippers take part in a somber Roman Catholic service on a street in Lima.

The Indians of the Amazon rain forest hold a variety of religious celebrations, which vary from tribe to tribe. Many of these observances involve prayers to the sun and moon. A religious leader, called a shaman, wears a feather headdress and has painted black stripes on his body, arms, and legs. He leads chants meant to keep the tribe in harmony with the forces that rule the universe. Some ceremonies involve driving out evil spirits or curing the sick.

The people of Peru also observe national religious holidays. Two of the most spectacular are celebrated with processions through the streets of Lima. On Santa Rosa de Lima Day and on the day honoring *El Señor de los Malagros*, or the "Lord of Miracles," a long and colorful parade to the cathedral ends in a solemn Mass. This is followed by music, street dances, and festive foods. Other religious holidays include Christmas, Easter, and All Saints' Day.

In addition to religious holidays, there are several national holidays that are patriotic observances similar to the Fourth of July in the United States. The most important is a double holiday: Independence Day on July 28 and National Day on July 29. This is an occasion for parades, speeches, fireworks, plus lots of holiday food and dancing.

Time to Eat

In Peru's cities and coastal farming regions, people enjoy a wide variety of foods. Rice, red beans, and meat or fish are common at the main meal. Some families still have this meal at midday, but for most, the main meal is enjoyed in the evening. One favorite dish in homes and in restaurants is *ceviche*, which is made of raw fish marinated in lemon juice. Another popular recipe is *Papa a la huancaína*—boiled potatoes

FROZEN ORANGE DELIGHT

*I*ngredients:

2 cups water
1 cup sugar
2 cups orange juice

1/4 cup lemon juice
grated rind of one orange

Measure the water into a saucepan and bring it to a boil. Stir in the sugar until it has dissolved completely. Allow the sweetened water to cool for about 20 minutes. Mix in the orange juice, lemon juice, and orange rind. Pour this mixture into two ice cube trays with the dividers removed, or use a freezer-proof bowl. Freeze until solid, and serve like ice cream or sherbet. Makes about two pints.

topped with a sauce made of milk, cheese, and chilis, and garnished with olives and hard-boiled eggs. The most common desserts are Peru's tropical fruits, which include oranges, bananas, avocados, and papayas.

The foods of the *sierra* highlands are much less varied. Indian families rely heavily on potatoes and corn. The highland farmers grow more than forty different varieties of potato. These are carefully separated, especially on market days, since each has a unique taste and texture.

One type of potato is used in a special way: The potatoes are spread on the ground overnight to freeze. The next day they thaw out. Repeated freezing and thawing produces a kind of powder, which is mixed in water to make a gruel. The result is *chuño* (CHEW-nyo). Served in soups or eaten plain, *chuño* is the most common food for many highland families.

Breakfast for the *sierra* families seldom varies. Among middle-class families it consists of two rolls shaped like triangles, coffee with lots of sugar, and a handful of roasted wheat kernels. Lunch is usually the same. The main meal, served after the day's work, is often a soup made with barley, corn, potatoes, and, of course, *chuño*. The family may occasionally have eggs or chicken, but meat is rarely served. *Ají,* or

City families often eat beans, which they can buy in markets like this one in Lima.

chili pepper, usually accompanies most meals. Children seldom have milk or fresh fruit, except on market day.

Two or three times a week, most highland families have a bowl of quinoa (KEEN-wa), which is served like a cooked cereal. Quinoa is a small, yellowish grain that has such a high protein content that it can take the place of meat in the diet. The Inca called it *chisiya ma*, "the mother grain." Today, government agricultural agents are urging the Andean people to eat more quinoa, along with two other high-protein native grains—*kiwicha* and *kaniwa*.

Clothing: Modern and Traditional

On the streets of Lima, or any other Peruvian city, people are dressed in clothing styles similar to those worn in North America. Here and there, however, one sees a shawl or poncho with bold stripes of dyed llama or alpaca wool—a reminder of Peru's Indian heritage.

On market day in a highland town in the Andes, the people are dressed in a variety of clothing. Many younger people wear modern clothes, such as jeans and sweaters. Girls and young women choose colorful skirts and dresses. Older people tend to prefer traditional clothing. The women wear long skirts, cotton blouses, and striking woolen shawls in colorful patterns. The ponchos worn by many men are woven in bright designs.

One of the most interesting articles of Indian clothing is the hat. Women as well as men wear straw or felt hats in a fedora or derby style, much like hats that some businessmen used to wear in the United States. Another hat style is a bowl-shaped woolen one. In ancient times, this type of hat was worn as a symbol of noble birth. Today Indian boys and men

Nearly everybody wears hats in the sierra—they're a favorite article of clothing. The three Indian men on the right are wearing fedoras, a popular style, with their striped woolen ponchos.

often wear colorful knit caps, some with long ear flaps that can be tied under the chin.

The Amazonian tribes of the tropical rain forest wear clothing suited to their hot, steamy environment. Most of their clothing consists of simple wrap-around pieces of cotton or woven grasses.

These girls attend a private school in the town of Chimbote, on the costa.

4
SCHOOL AND RECREATION

Eager to Learn, Happy to Play

All children in Peru are required to go to school from the age of six or seven until the age of sixteen. Schooling is free. One-quarter of the children, however, receive little or no education because there are not enough schools or teachers—especially in the remote highlands and rain forest.

Since 1980, the government has devoted large sums of money to building schools and training teachers. The problem continues, though, because the population is growing so fast. More than 40 percent of Peru's people are under the age of fifteen.

Peruvians take education seriously, and many Andean families will sacrifice a great deal to send their children to elementary school and high school. The average adult today has completed at least six years of school. About 75 percent of the people are literate—that is, they can read and write. This is one of the highest literacy rates in South America.

City Schools, Country Schools

If you lived in Lima, or in one of the other cities, you would go to elementary school from the age of six to the age of twelve, and then to secondary school until you were sixteen. While there are many public schools in the cities, most middle-class and upper-class families prefer to pay a tuition to send their children to private schools.

In most private schools, students wear uniforms—a skirt, blouse, and sweater for girls; slacks, white shirt, and a sweater or jacket for boys. Also, most private schools are operated by the Catholic Church. Public school students have religious classes as well, and these are taught by priests.

Children eat lunch with their teacher at a school in a mountain city.

Students listen attentively to their teacher at a high school in Arequipa, a city in southern Peru.

For elementary-school children in the cities, instruction is in Spanish. The subjects are similar to those taught in North American schools: grammar, reading, writing, history, geography, and some science. By third or fourth grade, children also study a foreign language, which is usually English. Some also learn Quechua.

The school year begins in the fall, usually in early February. There is a two-week winter vacation late in July. Summer vacation begins in late November or early December.

Let's imagine you live in the *sierra* highlands, where going to school is quite different. You walk more than a mile to

QUIPU: HISTORY ON STRINGS

In the Inca Empire, there was no written form of the Quechua language. The Inca did develop a remarkable system for keeping records, though. It was called a *quipu* (KI-pooh). A *quipu* was a set of strings of different lengths and colors, with knots placed at important points. The Inca used these strings to record information that helped the Inca rulers. With the help of the *quipu*, the Inca kept track of the number of people in a village, their dates of birth and death, crops grown, and the portion of their harvest paid to the emperor and to Inti, the sun god. Special scribes, called *quipu camayoc*, or "*quipu* readers," also used these devices to record the heroic deeds of each Inca ruler.

an elementary school in a small market town. The neatly dressed children line up outside the building in the chill mountain air—the girls on one side of the door, the boys on the other. School begins promptly at 9:00 A.M. The children are allowed to spank anyone who is late!

At home, you speak Quechua. Your parents know some Spanish, but your grandparents and many neighbors speak only Quechua. In school, all the lessons are in Spanish. You spend much of the classroom time learning to speak, read, and write in Spanish. You also study math and history. There are few books, so the teacher writes lessons on a large chalkboard for the children to copy or memorize. The school day ends at 12:30 P.M. so that you and the other children can help with the work at home.

Sometimes, the children board a bus for a field trip to one of the ancient Inca ruins. You have fun climbing on the huge square stones. The teacher explains that the people who built this place hundreds of years ago were your ancestors. This makes you feel very proud of your heritage.

When you are twelve, you will take a 20-mile bus ride every day through the Sacred Valley of the Inca to the nearest secondary school. Very few Indian children continue through the four years of secondary school. Even fewer have the chance to go to college. There are more than thirty colleges and universities in Peru. The National University of San Marcos, in Lima, was founded in 1551. It is believed to be the oldest in South America. Most Spanish young people and many mestizos are able to attend college.

Time for Fun

Peruvians along the Pacific Coast can enjoy the beaches throughout the year. And they don't have to worry about being caught in the rain. In most parts of the *costa*, including Lima, it seldom ever rains. Other kinds of outdoor fun are also possible in this mild coastal climate. Families enjoy picnics, walks through the parks, or visits to a bird sanctuary. In some sanctuaries in Peru, more than 500 species of birds have been identified.

In the evening, and on holidays, city families enjoy visiting friends or relatives. Usually these visits are unannounced, unless there is an invitation to dinner. When visitors arrive, the host family always offers them something to drink, such as coffee, juice, or soda. If the visitors come late in the afternoon, the family will usually serve a snack or light meal, which is called *lonche*.

City families enjoy watching television, going to the movies, and listening to the radio. Most movies and television programs are imported from Brazil, Argentina, or Mexico. Some are from the United States, usually with Spanish dubbed in. City children like to play board games and read comic books, and a growing number play video games.

Whether in the city or in the highlands, all children play soccer and volleyball. On playgrounds in Lima, on unpaved alleys in the shantytowns, and on the rocky hills of the *sierra*, soccer balls seem to be everywhere. In the *sierra*, Indian children sometimes play a game that is a combination

Everyone in Peru loves soccer—including these boys in Lima.

of soccer and volleyball. In families that rely on making woolen goods to earn a little extra money, it's not unusual to see children knitting and kicking a soccer ball around at the same time. The children in the *sierra* have no television sets and no access to movie theaters.

Every town in the Andes has an open-air market one day each week. The day varies from town to town. This allows people to sell goods in one town on Sunday, then go to a neighboring town for market day on Monday, and so on, through the week. Market day is a chance for children to play with friends, or simply to wander among the stalls of fruits and vegetables, woolen goods, and pottery.

Popular Pastimes

Soccer is by far the most popular sport for men. Women are more likely to play volleyball. Teams are organized by local clubs, called associations, in every coastal city. The games draw large crowds. Some of the rivalries between associations are fierce. Peru's national soccer team competes against other countries in World Cup matches and in the Olympic Games. Crowds of 70,000 fill Lima's National Stadium for international matches. Fans follow their favorite players closely on television and in newspaper reports.

Bullfighting is popular in towns and cities along the Pacific Coast. Large crowds come to the famous Plaza de Acho in Lima for the colorful and dramatic fights. To Peruvians, and to many people in other Latin American countries, bullfights are an ancient and honorable tradition. Horse racing, basketball, and baseball are becoming more popular every year. Some Peruvians also venture into the Andes for skiing.

Peru has many skilled craftspeople, including this woman, who is selling her jewelry and hand carved gourds at an outdoor market.

5
THE ARTS

Building on Great Traditions

The art, music, and crafts of Peru grow out of the two great traditions—the Indian tradition of the Inca and pre-Inca cultures, and the Spanish tradition, which came to Peru in the 1500s. These traditions remain mostly separate and distinct. But there is a growing mestizo culture that blends the customs of both.

Crafts, Past and Present

Peru's Indian heritage in crafts is one of the oldest in the world. In the ruins of ancient cities and towns, and in tombs, archeologists have found outstanding examples of weaving, pottery, and metalwork. These objects were made over a period of more than 2,000 years. Over the centuries, one Indian civilization after another developed its own unique artistic designs. Modern Indian craftspeople have kept alive the great art forms of their ancestors.

Peru's Andean Indians are best known for their weaving. They use yarns that are made from the fleece of sheep and

An elderly hatmaker works next to his open shop door. Hats are very popular in Peru.

of four animal species that belong to the camel family: llama, alpaca, guanaco, and vicuña.

The Indians weave these soft yarns into fabrics with bright stripes on which they sometimes embroider designs. The cloth is then made into blankets, sweaters, ponchos, shawls, and wall hangings, all in a rainbow of vivid colors. On market day in every town, there are always colorful displays of these handwoven items. In coastal regions, mestizo weavers use Peru's world-famous cotton to make dazzling new fabric designs that reflect both Spanish and Indian styles.

Pottery is another Peruvian craft with a long, proud tradition. Beautiful bowls, bottles, and jars found in Inca and pre-Inca ruins are displayed in museums throughout the world. Some of these objects are considered among the finest of their kind ever made. Modern Indian potters continue to use their skills to make outstanding dishes, bowls, and finely crafted beads for necklaces.

Inca and pre-Inca metalwork, especially in gold and silver, was also skillfully done. Unfortunately, some of the finest examples of metalworking were seized by the Spanish conquerors, who had these objects melted down into bars of gold and silver. Although much has been lost, the Museum of Gold in Lima has thousands of goblets, ornaments, and jewelry that display the great skills of the crafters. Modern metalworkers continue to fashion ornamental objects and jewelry, but copper has replaced gold.

The ancient peoples of Peru left behind examples of their beautiful handicrafts, such as this clay jar.

MACHU PICCHU: THE LOST CITY

Around 1911, a scientist from the United States named Hiram Bingham went in search of Inca ruins. After months of disappointment, a *campesino* led him through dense jungle up a mountain that the farmer called Machu Picchu (mah-CHOOH PEE-chu). Near the summit, Bingham found himself staring in amazement at the ruins of an entire city spread out between two jagged peaks. There were hundreds of stone houses, a fortress, and great temples. The site covered more than 5 square miles (13 square kilometers). It included terraced farm plots and gardens connected by 3,000 stone steps cut out of solid rock.

Some scholars believe that Machu Picchu was a royal estate of the emperor Pachacuti. But no one really knows exactly when the Inca lived there, or how the Spanish conquerors missed it. Most mysterious of all, no one knows why this "lost city" was abandoned.

Some of the 3,000 stone steps in Machu Picchu are visible in this photograph.

Architecture

Some of the most spectacular achievements of the Inca and pre-Inca cultures were their works made of stone. Walls, temples, fortresses, and palaces were built of massive blocks of stone. The blocks were fitted together so perfectly that no cement or mortar was needed to hold them in place. Many of these structures have survived centuries of earthquakes. Tourists and scholars from all over the world come to gaze in wonder at these silent monuments to Peru's history.

The stone blocks of this Inca wall fit together so perfectly that the wall has lasted through the centuries, even though no mortar was used to strengthen it.

Peru has more ruins of ancient stone structures than any country in South America. New sites are still being uncovered, while some remain hidden in the desert of the *costa* or in the heavy forests on the eastern slopes of the Andes Mountains.

The Spanish brought European architecture to Peru in the sixteenth century. Every city has examples of ornate Spanish cathedrals, churches, palaces, and public buildings. Their interiors are decorated with beautiful murals, statues, and elaborate chandeliers. After much of Lima was destroyed by an earthquake in 1746, many buildings were erected in more modern European styles. Today, Peru's architects work in steel, concrete, and glass, just as architects do in cities all over the world.

Music and Dance

The music and dance of Peru reflect the nation's rich and varied cultural heritage. On radios and tape decks, young people listen to the latest rock releases from North America and Europe. Older Peruvians prefer traditional music, including classical music by European and South American composers, and the ancient Indian music of the Andes.

Andean Indians who have moved to the cities form associations, or clubs, with others who come from the same district of the highlands. The associations meet at least once a week. Members prepare foods from their region and spend the evening doing lively folk dances. Some of the members provide the music. They play drums, rattles, and sometimes a harp. Usually someone plays a row of flutes tied together, called an *antara*, and someone else plays a *charango*, a string instrument like a guitar.

An Amazonian Indian plays the flute near his home in the rain forest.

PERU IN ARTS AND LETTERS

Ricardo Palma (1833–1919), the first great writer in Peru. His novels, including *Knights of the Cape*, were collections of humorous stories about life during the colonial period.

Clorinda Matto de Turner (c. 1850–1921), the first Peruvian author to write about the lives of the Indian people. Her most famous novel, *Birds Without a Nest*, was published in 1889.

José Sabogal (1888–1956), regarded as Peru's finest artist. He was best known for his sympathetic attitude toward the Indians.

César Vallejo (1895–1938), considered Peru's greatest poet. His collections of poetry, such as *Human Poems*, explored social concerns—especially poverty.

Mario Vargas Llosa (1936–   ), Peru's best-known modern author. His novels have been widely read throughout the world. They include *The City and the Dogs*, *The Green House*, and *Aunt Julia and the Scriptwriter*. Vargas Llosa is a passionate spokesperson for democracy. He even made an unsuccessful bid for the presidency.

Mestizo music is different and very popular. Live bands play in cafés and dance halls. The instruments are the same as those used by the Indians, with the addition of guitars, wood-winds, horns, and sometimes a violin. Special nightclubs, called *peñas* (PAYN-yahs), play only folk music—usually mestizo tunes.

Folk dances are part of every celebration, from birthdays and weddings to week-long festivals. Dancers wear feather headdresses on wooden frames, which they tie to their hats. Music is supplied by drums and flutes, and occasionally by brass instruments. The dance movements are spontaneous rather than formal. Groups form and dissolve during a dance, then re-form again, and sometimes expand to include everyone. Dancers often lead a procession to church for the celebration of Mass during festivals.

Literature and Art

Since there was no written form of the Quechua language, the Inca relied on telling their stories and legends. Each generation handed the tales down to the next generation. Many of these oral tales, including proverbs and superstitions, are still told in the mountain villages.

When the Spanish arrived, they were fascinated by the achievements of the Inca. A number of Spanish writers recorded some of the Inca stories, legends, and myths. They also created an alphabet and dictionary for Quechua.

In the late nineteenth century, Clorinda Matto de Turner began writing about the life of the Andean Indians. Her stories were very popular, and many novelists who came after her explored the same theme. A number of modern writers have focused on the conflict between the Indians and the upper classes of Peruvian society. These novels have made people of Spanish descent and mestizos more aware of the problems Indians face in trying to escape generations of poverty.

Painting and sculpture, like literature, developed during the colonial period. Spanish artists created outstanding paintings and murals to decorate cathedrals, churches, public buildings, and the grand homes of the wealthy. During the seventeenth and eighteenth centuries, Peruvian artists developed their own special style that became known as the Cuzco School. Modern painters and sculptors have worked in more abstract forms. Like so much else in Peru, the nation's art reflects the rich heritage of its Indian and Spanish inhabitants.

Country Facts

Official Name: República del Perú (Republic of Peru)

Capital: Lima

Location: Peru is located on the west coast of South America, just south of the equator. The country is bordered by Ecuador and Colombia on the north, Brazil and Bolivia on the east, Chile on the south, and the Pacific Ocean on the west.

Area: 296,223 square miles (1,285,218 square kilometers). *Greatest distances:* east–west, 875 miles (1,408 kilometers); north–south, 1,225 miles (1,971 kilometers). *Coastline:* 1,448 miles (2,330 kilometers).

Elevation: *Highest:* Mount Huascarán in west central Peru, 22,205 feet (6,768 meters). *Lowest:* sea level.

Climate: Although the northern border of Peru nearly touches the equator, the coastal climate is kept fairly cool by the Peru Current. The coast is also one of the driest regions in the world. In the Andes Mountains, temperatures vary with the altitude. The *selva* of eastern Peru is Amazon rain forest with hot temperatures year-round and 90 inches (227 centimeters) or more of rain every year.

Population: 23.6 million. *Distribution:* 70 percent urban; 30 percent rural.

Form of Government: democratic republic

Important Products: *Natural resources:* copper, iron ore, silver, zinc, gold, lead, petroleum, natural gas, hydroelectric power, guano (seabird droppings widely used for fertilizer), and nitrate. *Agriculture:* sugarcane, coffee, cotton, corn, potatoes, rice, wheat, beans, and barley. Livestock include sheep, cattle, pigs, llamas, alpacas, guanaco, and vicuna. *Industries:* fishing, cement, automobile and truck assembly, food processing, furniture, and tires. Handicraft industries include weaving, pottery, jewelry making, and metalworking.

Basic Unit of Money: sol; 1 sol = 100 centavos.

Language: Spanish, Quechua, and Aymara are all official languages. Tribes of the Amazon rain forest speak several languages.

Religion: 90 percent Roman Catholic. Andean Indians often combine Catholicism with Inca and other ancient beliefs. There are small numbers of Protestants, Jews, and Buddhists.

Flag: three vertical stripes: red, white, and red. In the center is the national coat of arms, containing symbols of Peru's abundance of plants, animals, and minerals.

National Anthem: Himno Nacional ("National Hymn")

Major Holidays: New Year's Day (January 1); Easter Weekend (date varies); Labor Day (May 1); Day of the Peasant (June 24); Independence Day and National Day (July 28 and 29); St. Rose of Lima Day (August 30); All Saints' Day (November 1); Immaculate Conception (December 8); Christmas (December 25).

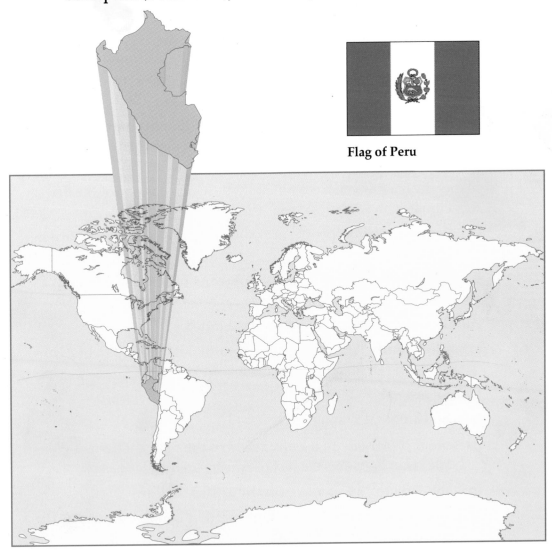

Flag of Peru

Peru in the World

Glossary

adobe: clay-like mud formed into bricks and dried in the sun

alpaca: An animal that is related to the camel and has long, silky wool.

antara: a cluster of flutes of different lengths tied together; also known as a panpipe

archaeologist: a person who studies the remains of ancient civilizations

Aymara: a large Indian tribe living primarily in southern Peru in the area of Lake Titicaca; also the ancient language spoken there

campesinos: Indians who live by farming

charango: a stringed instrument, similar to a guitar, used for playing the music of the Andean Indians

chuño: potatoes that have been frozen and thawed until they form a powder, from which a gruel is made; a common food among Indians of the Andes

costa: the narrow coastal plain of Peru, which has one of the driest climates on earth

Creoles, or *Criollos:* people of Spanish descent who were born in Peru

descent: describes one's origins. Someone of Spanish descent has ancestors who were Spanish.

endangered: in danger of becoming extinct

extended family: the large family unit that includes parents, children, grandparents, aunts, uncles, and cousins

feria: a festival

fleece: an animal's woolly coat

hacienda: a plantation; usually refers to the Spanish-owned plantations in Peru and the rest of South America

irrigate: to supply water to crops by artificial means

kaniwa: a grain with a very high protein content grown in the Andes *kiwicha:* an Andean mountain grain, rich in protein

mestizo (meh-STEE-zoh): people of mixed Spanish and Indian ancestry, making up about 37 percent of the population of Peru

montaña: the eastern foothills of the Andes, including the lower *selva,* or Amazon rain forest; the region covers more than half of Peru

nomads: people who have no permanent home and who move often to find fresh food supplies and pasture for their animals

Quechua (ket-CHOO-ah): the language of the ancient Inca, which is still an official language and is spoken by many Peruvians

quinoa (KEEN-wa): a grain with a very high protein content, grown by many Andean Indians

selva: the rain forest of eastern Peru

sierra: the highlands and mountains of the Andes

For Further Reading

Chrisp, Peter. *The Incas*. New York: Thomson Learning, 1994.

Falconer, Kieran. *Peru*. New York: Marshall Cavendish, 1995.

Karpfinger, Beth. *Peru Is My Home*. New York: Gareth Stevens, 1993.

Lepthein, Emile U. *Peru*. Chicago: Children's Press, 1992.

Lye, Keith. *Take a Trip to Peru*. New York: Edwin Watts, 1987.

Mangurian, David. *Children of the Incas*. New York: Four Winds Press, 1979.

Peru in Pictures. Minneapolis, MN: Lerner Publications, 1987.

St. John, Jetty. *A Family in Peru*. Minneapolis, MN: Lerner Publications, 1987.

Index

Page numbers for illustrations are in boldface

About the Author

"One of the great things about books is that they can carry us to every corner of the world. We can also travel back in time, visiting people and places from recent years or the distant past. I hope you enjoy this book's journey across both space and time," says David C. King.

Mr. King is a historian and an author, who has written more than thirty books for young readers. In addition to books about foreign countries, he has written stories and biographies in American history. He and his wife, Sharon Flitterman-King, live in the village of Hillsdale, New York. They welcome visitors.